MADEIRA

THE ISLAND OF FLOWERS

Arco do São Jorge

TRAVEL GUIDE

Baltasar Rodriguez Oteros

Levada da Serra do Faial

INDEX

Madeira, the island of Flowers, has the most spectacular and beautiful landscapes in Portugal and one of the most beautiful in the world.

How to get to Madeira?

The airline TAP Portugal has eight direct flights a day from Lisbon to Cristiano Ronaldo International Airport (because this beautiful island is the homeland of the famous international soccer player). Between the Portuguese capital and the archipelago it takes approximately 1 to 45 minutes to travel.

The airport is located **16 km from Funchal.**

There is a bus every hour from the terminal to the city center with a journey time of 15 minutes.

Madeira needs 7 days to be able to be visited with ease and get to know all its beautiful towns, beaches, volcanoes and monuments.

The probability of rain is low in all months, being the rainiest in November, in addition, the average temperature throughout the year is 20°C.

Funchal

It is the capital of the island of Madeira.

We can see its beautiful gardens and parks, the cobblestone streets with beautiful decorative mosaics, the colonial-style houses with intense colors and wooden balconies.

In the central square is the building of the **Town Hall,** former **Palace of Count Caravalhal** from the 18th century.

From this square and continuing along Rua do Bispo, we reach the **Episcopal Palace,** seat of the Museum of Sacred Art.

On Avenida Arraiga is the **Municipal Theater** Baltazar Días.

It has two castles that protected it from pirate incursions: **Forte do Pico and Forte do Santiago** from the 17th century, the latter in the port area, it houses the Museum of Contemporary Art.

From **Forte de Santiago** you can contemplate the imposing Atlantic Ocean.

Going up the Funchal cable car you will be able to see an impressive sunset.

The **Mercado dos Lavradores,** is a traditional market with all kinds of local and artisan products.

Mercado dos Lavradores

Palácio dos Cônsules, Funchal

In the **Monte Palace Tropical Garden** you can admire all the subtropical flora of the island of Las Flores. You can visit the **Museo da Quinta das Cruzes.**

Funchal Cathedral (Largo da Se)

Built in 1514 by order of King D. Manuel I, it is its most visited monument.

The tower is covered with tiles.

The royal coat of arms appears on the main porch with the cross of the Knights Templar, of which the king was the Grand Master of the Order.

The ceiling is covered with a coffered ceiling wood and ivory.

In the choir are the sculptures of the 12 Apostles painted gold with a blue background.

The silver processional cross, offered by King Manuel I, is considered one of the masterpieces of Portuguese goldsmithing.

Schedule:

Every day from 9:00 a.m. to 12:00 p.m. and from 4:00 p.m. to 5:30 p.m.

Free entrance
(+351) 291 228 155.

Santa Clara Convent
Calçada de Santa Clara 15
Built during the fifteenth century, with the most beautiful pottery on the island, beautiful Portuguese Mudejar-style tiles.

Palace of San Lorenzo (Forte de São Lourenço)
Zarco Avenue
Manueline-style palace-fortress. Construction began during the reign of Manuel I, and was completed under Philip I of Portugal (Philip II of Spain).

It was the official residence of the captains, headquarters of the military garrison, and residence of the governor until in 1836 it was divided into a fortress and a palace; a part is occupied by the Madeira Military Command; the other is the residence of the

Minister of the Autonomous Region of Madeira.

Here you can see the Noble Room, the Audience Room and the Green Room; in addition to its beautiful gardens.

Inside is the Military Museum of Madeira, where a wide collection of weapons and artillery pieces is exhibited.

Schedule:
From Tuesday to Friday from 10:00 a.m. to 12:00 p.m. and from 2:00 p.m. to 5:00 p.m.
Saturday from 10:00 a.m. to 12:00 p.m. Closed holidays.
Price. €2

Fortress of São João Baptista or São João do Pico.
It is located in Funchal at 111 meters above sea level.

It was built in the 17th century as an arsenal and later as a military barracks where in the 20th century the army's communications antennas were installed.
of gunpowder in the city.
The entire history of this castle is on display in the small museum.
Rua do Castelo.

Schedule:
Every day from 9:00 a.m. to 6:00 p.m.
Free entrance.

Fort of Santiago
Fortress built in the 17th century to defend the port.
It is located in the historic city center.

Visiting hours:
Monday to Friday from 9:30 a.m. to 3:30 p.m.

Closed on Saturdays, Sundays and holidays.
You have to pay entrance.

Madeira Botanical Garden Eng.º Rui Vieira

It is located 3 km from **Funchal (Santa Maria Maior)** between 150
and 300 meters above sea level. It measures 8 hectares in size.
With more than 2,000 species of subtropical plants and flowers, it
is one of the most beautiful botanical gardens in the world.
In the enclosure you will be able to see centennial Dragos, typical
of all the islands, all the species of cacti and orchids that you can
imagine.

The flower beds form geometric drawings of infinite colors. There is a Japanese Garden in Monte Palace and its lake.

Bus lines no. 29, 30, 31 and 31A
(http://www.horariosdofunchal.pt.) arrive there.
You can also use the cable car to Largo das Babosas (Monte) station.
http://www.telefericojardimbotanico.com
The entry of bicycles, scooters and pets is prohibited, except guide dogs accompanying the blind.
Children must always be accompanied by an adult.

Schedule
From Monday to Sunday, from 9:00 a.m. to 6:00 p.m.
(last ticket sold at 5:30 p.m.).
Closed on December 25.

Entrance through the main door, next to the cable car station, (north area of the garden).

The entrance ticket is unique and allows you to visit the garden areas and the Museum of Natural History.

The Garden has rest areas with seats and several viewpoints with views of the port of Funchal.

The ticket expires when the visitor leaves the premises (they cannot re-enter).

The time to go through the entire garden is 2 hours.

Prices until December 31, 2022

General admission (visitors over 12 years old): €6

Reduced ticket (visitors aged between 6 and 12 years): €2

Free admission: Children under 6 years old.

As of January 1, 2023.

General admission (visitors over 12 years old): €7.50.

Reduced ticket (visitors aged between 6 and 12 years): €3

Free admission: Children under 6 years old, April 30 (Anniversary

of the Madeira Botanical Garden), July 1 (Day of the Madeira Autonomous Region)
For a guided tour by garden staff or use for events, you must consult the visitor service center (Portaria).

Site accessibility
The trails are not adapted for the use of wheelchairs, and the unevenness of the terrain can present difficulties for people with reduced mobility.
Caminho do Meio, Bom Sucesso Funchal – Madeira
(+351) 291211200
Fax (+351) 291211206
Email: ifcn@madeira.gov.pt

Cable Car (To the Botanical Garden)

Funicular Station Ticket Office

Price
-Adults
A single trip (round trip): €9.25
Round trip: €14.00
-From 7 to 14
A single trip (round trip): €4.50
Round trip: €7.00
-6 years or less: free.

Hours:
9 a.m. to 5 p.m. (January 1, 10:30 a.m. to 5 p.m.)

Monte Palace Tropical Garden
The 7-hectare garden has all the subtropical varieties of the laurel

forest, such as the extremely rare Madeira agar; the Japanese garden with all kinds of oriental decoration; a collection of minerals and gems, and another collection of sculptures.

montepalace.com
Caminho do Monte, 174. Or Caminho das Babosas, 4, Funchal.

Schedule:
The garden is open from Monday to Friday from 9:00 a.m. to 6:00 p.m.
The museum is open daily from 10:30 a.m. to 4:30 p.m.
Closed on December 25.
You can go up by cable car, taxi or buses 20, 21, 22, 48.
Ticket price: 10 euros per person (under 15 years, free).

A Madeira wine tasting is included with admission. The ticket can be used as a postcard.

Along the paths that run through the garden, the entire history of Portugal is told in beautiful tiles.

It has an **amphora** that is 5 meters high and weighs more than 500 kg, the largest in the world, registered in the **Guinness Book of Records.**

Madeira Wine Museum (Adegas de São Francisco)

It is located inside the old monastery of San Francisco and houses bottles from 1860,

and the oak barrels that, together with the special climate of the island, give the wine its special flavor that is highly appreciated. Here you can learn about the entire production process. The visit ends with a tasting of these aromatic wines of recognized varieties such as Mole, Malvasia, Verdelho, Sercial...

28 Arriaga Avenue
Guided tours €4.20.

Schedule:
Open Monday through Friday from 9:30 a.m. to 6:30 p.m. with guided tours at 10:30 a.m., 2:30 p.m., 3:30 p.m. and 4:30 p.m. Saturdays from 10:00 a.m. to 1:00 p.m., with a guided tour at 11:00 a.m.
Sundays closed.

Funchal Toy Museum (Museu do Brinquedo)
It exhibits the collection of old toys of José Manuel Borges Pereira.
It has a cafe/restaurant.
Rua da Levada dos Barreiros, 48.

Schedule:
Open from Tuesday to Saturday from 10:00 a.m. to 6:30 p.m.
Sundays from 12:30 p.m. to 6:30 p.m.
(+351) 919 922 722.

Cristiano Ronaldo Museum (Museum CR7)
It is located next to the **port of Funchal.**
This museum opened in 2013 has 1,400 m² and exhibits all the trophies, ballon d'or and golden boots; all junior and professional trophies won in the clubs of CF Andorinha, Nacional da Madeira, Sporting CP, Manchester United, Real Madrid, Juventus FC and the Portugal national team, more than 126 obetos of the great

footballer from Madeira, a life-size statue of Cristiano Ronaldo, gigantic photographs and iconic video.

Rua Princesa D. Amelia, 10

Schedule:
From Monday to Saturday from 10:00 a.m. to 6:00 p.m.
Ticket price: €5.
Free entry for children up to 9 years old.
+351 291 639 880.

Madeira Casino
Infante Avenue
(+351) 291 209 180)
It is the only casino on the island, designed by the famous Brazilian architect Oscar Niemeyer, designer of the city of Brasilia (capital of Brazil).

Museum of the Quinta das Cruzes

The 18th century building houses the invaluable art collection: furniture, ceramics, sculpture, porcelain, jewellery... by César Filipe Gomes, a prestigious Madeiran collector.

In the enclosure there is the chapel of Nossa Senhora da Piedade, an archaeological park and the orchid garden.

The English Chippendale and Sheraton furniture stands out, or Portuguese furniture made with precious woods (sugar box) Porcelain pieces from Meissen, Saxe, Limoges..., clay figures for Christmas decoration from the 18th century.

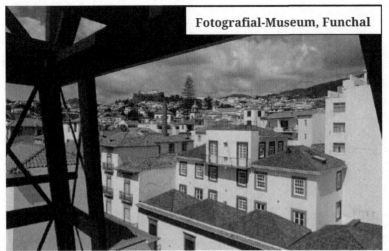

Fotografial-Museum, Funchal

Santa Catarina-Park

Câmara do Lobos (Chamber of Wolves)

Fishing village with small traditional houses next to modern buildings and recreational and leisure areas.

They say it is the most beautiful fishing village in Madeira.

Cabo Girao and its cliffs

To the south of the island is the highest cliff in Europe and the second in the world, with 580 meters above sea level. From here you can look into the void from a glass platform. In its surroundings is the **Chapel of Our Lady of Fatima.**
Be sure to see this cliff from afar.

Ribeira Brava

It is a small fishing village with a picturesque market of traditional products, the church of Sao Bento and the tower near the maritime avenue. It is located in a valley (Ribeira Brava ravine) surrounded by plantations of sugar cane and tropical fruits.
Be sure to visit its botanical garden with flowers, trees and all kinds of plants.
On June 29, the patron saint festivities are celebrated in honor of San Pedro.

Gorgulho Beach, with beautiful views of the island, is a quiet family beach.

Ponta do Sol

Its crystal clear turquoise waters and an old shipwreck, the Bow Belle, have made it a diving paradise.

In **Ponta do Sol** we can see the crops of sugar cane and its beautiful beaches.

Calheta Beach

It is the most visited town on the island, due to its beautiful artificial beach with fine white sand, probably the best in Madeira, the marina and the long maritime avenue.

Here you can visit the Engenhos da Calheta Distilleries, where the best rum on the island is made.

Other Beaches

Madeira has black sand beaches, small rocky beaches and natural pools with crystal clear waters.

Formosan beach

Located near Funchal. It is a beach of rock and sand very frequented by people from the island.

Prainha

(To the east of the island) is one of the fine sand beaches that Madeira has, where volcanic sand beaches abound.

Jardim do Mar Beach

This rocky beach, on the edge of the laurel forest, is a paradise for surfers.

Punta do Pargo

The Ponta do Pargo lighthouse is the most beautiful on the island.

Faja dos Padres Beach
Located in the **south** of the island. You get here by ascending and descending through a picturesque elevator.

Porto Moniz
In the northwest of the island, 15 minutes by car from San Vicente, is Porto Moniz, a fishing village where its natural seawater pools stand out, the best known on the entire island.
Its facilities have all the services (changing rooms, children's areas, restaurants, parking lots...).
Nearby is the Mole islet, on which there is a lighthouse.
Madeira has both pebbly and black-sand beaches, and this stunning lagoon is ideal for a relaxing swim.

In Porto Moniz there is also the **Sao Joao Baptista Castle,** built in the 18th century.

Porto Moniz

Seixal

Other natural pools are those of **Ponta Gorda, Ponta Delgada, Ponta Gorda, Seixal and Faial.**

Live Science Center

In **Porto Moniz** you will find this interesting interactive museum for the whole family, with a large auditorium.

Rotunda do Ilheu Mole, Porto Moniz

Schedule:

From Tuesday to Sunday from 10:00 a.m. to 7:00 p.m.

(+351) 291 850 305.

E-mail: info@ccvportominiz.com

Madeira Aquarium

It is located in **Porto Moniz** in the São João Baptista fortress, built in 1730 to repel pirate attacks.

With more than 90 native species in 12 gigantic pools.

Here you can dive among all kinds of marine animals, making your visit a unique experience.

Schedules:

From Monday to Sunday, from 10:00 a.m. to 6:00 p.m.

Single Ticket: €8

General Admission: €7

Group ticket (from 5 people): €5.

Children between 5 and 14 years old: €4.

From 65 years: €4.

Groups of people over 65 years old (from 5 people): €3

Sao Vicente

With its caves and a volcano museum, where you can learn more about the formation of this island.

Caves of Sao Vicente
The tunnels through which the lava flowed more than 400,000 years ago created these caves with a length of 700 metres, where you can see impressive stalactites and stalactites, and some

archaeological remains.

Pé do Passo site
Schedule:
Every day from 10:00 a.m. to 7:00 p.m.
Ticket price: €8 per adult.

Santana

Located in the northeast of the island, this small and beautiful fishing village preserves some of the houses with the traditional architecture of Madeira (**palheiros**). They are houses painted in intense colors with sloping roofs in the shape of a triangle and thatched roof. one of the most typical postcards and one of the most visited places on the island of the Island.

Some of these picturesque houses (**Casinhas de Santana**) have been transformed into a museum and can be visited by the public. From this town you can enter the greenery of the surrounding Laurisilva Forest.

In Santana, its impressive cliffs also stand out.

Santana Park-Museum

You can see a replica of the Monte train, ox carts, Santana houses, mills, a labyrinth and a lake.

Regional State 101, Fonte da Pedra, **Santana**

Hours: From 10:00 a.m. to 7:00 p.m.

Price

Adults: €10.

Over 65s: €8.

Children and young people from 5 to 14 years old: €8.

Islets of Ribeira Da Janela

Less than ten minutes by car from **Porto Moniz** are the Islets of Ribeira Da Janela, one of the most picturesque images of Madeira, facing its black rock beaches.

Island of Porto Santo

Porto Santo and its beautiful beaches of fine sand.
Northwest of Madeira is the island of Porto Santo, the second largest island in the archipelago.

House of Christopher Columbus

Here is the **house of Christopher Columbus.**

Unlike **Madeira**, the Island of **Porto Santo** does have long and extensive beaches of fine sand.
Porto Santo beach is 9 km long and has the finest white sand with crystal clear turquoise waters.
Its waves are a paradise for the most experienced surfers.
Every morning a ferry leaves the port of Funchal for Porto Santo and returns in the late afternoon.

Ferry from Porto Santo to Funchal
The journey takes 2 hours and 15 minutes and the trip costs between €50 and €74, if you board with a rental car.

Santa Cruz

A 15-minute drive from Fuchal, in the airport area of the island, is Santa Cruz with some beautiful beaches.

Aqua Park

Water park located in **Santa Cruz** with capacity for more than 1,000 people, swimming pools, 3 water-slides, 4 fast tracks, 1 fast river, 1 black-hole, 1 hole river, 1 lazy river, 1 leisure pool and a children's aqualandia.

Schedule:
From 10:00 a.m. to 6:00 p.m.
Prices
Adults: €10
Children (from 5 to 12 years old): €7
Children up to 4 years old: Free admission.
(+351) 291640535.
E-mail: geral@aquaparque.com

Machico

12 minutes from **Santa Cruz** is **Machico**, with a 15th century church, the **Forte de Nossa Senhora do Amparo** and the **Forte de Sao Joao Baptista,** two castles that protected the coast and the city.

Forte de Nossa Senhora do Amparo

Near **Machico** is the viewpoint of **Pico de Facho and Ponto do Buraco.**

Curral das Freiras

In a deep ravine located in the center of the island, is Curral das Freiras, surrounded by impressive mountains.

In this place the inhabitants of the island took refuge when the coast was attacked by pirate ships.

Levadas

This extensive network of ancient canals (levadas) that runs through the entire island, began to be built in the 16th century.

Through these canals they carry water from the top of the mountains to the lower areas. This network of canals is traveled by many hikers, as Madeira is a trekking paradise with all kinds of routes.

Levada do Caniçal

The southern part of the island, much drier and more populated, had for centuries extensive plantations of sugar cane, bananas or vineyards, which produce the appreciated Madeira wine.
In the north and northwest of the island, the trade winds move the clouds along the slopes of the high mountains where the laurel forests retain and condense moisture, creating numerous streams such as the Ribeira Brava stream that rises in the Serra de Agua. . This ingenious system of canals carries water from one area to another on the island and is 1,400 kilometers long.

100 kilometers built at 1000 meters of altitude, serve to supply four hydroelectric plants.

This network runs through the interior of the island and along some cliffs.

Caldeirão Verde (Green Caldeirao)

Near **Santana**, there are the 2.2 kilometer Caldeirão Verde trails that cross the **Queimadas Park**, entering the dense laurel forests between deep valleys and ravines through which torrents of water fall.

A paradise of greenery and peace.

Caldeirão Verde Trail

It is another of the most popular hiking trails.

The vehicle is parked at **Casa dos Queimadas**, where there is a lodging and visitor center.

Between leafy forests, after going through some tunnels and

traveling 6 km, you reach Caldeirao Verde, a waterfall with an 80-meter drop that creates a small lagoon.

Levada do Caldeirão Verde

Laurissilva-forest

| Levada do Caldeirão Verde | Santa Luzia, Funchal |

25 Fontes and the Risco.

It is the most visited levada on the island. The **Velha do Rabaçal** levada, built between 1835 and 1860, is the starting point that begins at the Rabaçal refuge, which is accessed after crossing

Paul de la Serra, the only flat place of the island.

-In Rabaçal there is the Wind Lagoon (**Lagoa do Vento**), and **Risco**, from where you can see the waterfall that originates the water of the lake. From there there are about 4.5 km of narrow path to the 25 Fontes, with its high walls of volcanic rock through which numerous torrents emerge.

-Another path connects with **Porto Moniz**. El Rabaçal is 300 meters higher.

Cascada Risco/RiscoWaterfall

Viewpoints

In the north of the island there are numerous viewpoints.

Ponta do Pargo viewpoint

It is located in the north of the island, at the westernmost point of Madeira, and from here you can see some beautiful views, as well

as the lighthouse that is still in operation.
It is probably the most spectacular viewpoint of the whole island.
From this place you will be able to see an unforgettable sunset.

Ponta de Sao Lourenco Viewpoint

In the southeast of the island, 30 minutes by car from Funchal, between **Santa Cruz** and **Machico**, very close to the airport, is the viewpoint with the most impressive views of the entire island.

Here there are 9 kilometers of reddish cliffs jutting out into the sea, a narrow reddish strip of land that seems to disappear in the waves.

On clear days you can see the island of **Porto Santo** and the small **Desertas Islands**.

Rocha do Navio viewpoint

Located in **Santana** with an impressive view of the cliffs, a small waterfall and wild volcanic rock beaches.

A cable car leads to the highest part of the cliff.

Balcões viewpoint

You can only get here by walking 30 to 45 minutes along a path of low-medium difficulty.

If there are no clouds over the mountains, the views are unspeakable.

Cabo Girão viewpoint

 Incredible views of the Atlantic Ocean. In an area of the viewpoint there is a glass platform over the enormous abyss that is not suitable for those who suffer from vertigo, an experience that will make you vibrate without limit.

Garajau and Christ the King

To the east of Funchal is the Garajau point, with the spectacular

53

Pinaculo Viewpoint and the impressive image of the Christ of Garajau that seems to be hanging in the abyss.

Pinaculo Lookout
It is located near **Funchal**, the capital of the island, and from this point there is a magnificent view of the city.
The car park is small so you may have to wait a bit to park your rental car.

Rosario Lookout
Overlooking **Machico**, situated in the middle of a valley, and close to the island's airport.
It is the ideal place to see the planes landing and taking off from the nearby Madeira Airport (Cristiano Ronaldo). Landing is sometimes difficult, and from here you can see the maneuvers of

the pilots.

Pico do Facho Viewpoint

Pico do Facho is the highest point of the island of **Porto Santo** with 517 meters of altitude.

From its top a bonfire was lit to warn of pirate attacks and could be seen from the Ponta do São Lourenço on the island of Madeira. The road that leads to its summit begins in Vila Baleira.

Pico do Arieiro Viewpoint.

It is the third highest peak on the island, its viewpoint is located at 1818 meters high.

You have to leave the vehicle in the designated parking lot at the bottom of the mountain, and walk up the marked path.
You can enjoy sensational views from its viewpoint.

Pico Ruivo (Ruivo Peak)

From Santana, in the north of the island, there is a winding road that crosses the Queimadas Park and reaches a spectacular viewpoint. Continuing along the same road, we reach the Pico Ruivo peak, the highest point on the island at 1,862 meters. .
It can be ascended by a path of medium difficulty.

Before starting the ascent on foot, you have to leave the car in a large parking lot.
They say that from Pico Ruivo on a clear day you can see **Mount Teide** in **Tenerife (Canary Islands)**.

Boca Encumeada

Natural Parks

-The **Desertas Islands Nature Reserve: Ilhéu Chão, Deserta Grande and Bugio** is the last refuge in the Atlantic for the monk seal (Monachus monachus).

To visit Deserta Grande you need a special permit from the Madeira Natural Park Services.

-The **Wild Islands Nature Reserve: Selvagem Grande, Selvagem Pequena and Ilhéu de Fora**. Here is a refuge for birds and numerous endemic botanical species, which are only found on this island.

-The **Garajau Nature Reserve** stands out for its beautiful seabed full of marine life.

-In **Santana**, to the north of the island, is the **Rocha do Navio Nature Reserve**, with the islets of Rocha das Vinhas and Viúva.

-The **Dragoeiros das Neves**, located in **São Gonçalo,** with its beautiful garden where the centenary dragon trees are found.

The Cascade of the 25 Fountains
It is located in **Ribeira da Janela,** near **Porto Moniz**
It has a drop of 30 meters high that ends in a lagoon.

The Bridal Veil Waterfall (Véu da Noiva)
It is located near **Seixal (Porto Moniz)**.

The water falls directly into the Atlantic Ocean after going down a cliff near the old **R 101 highway,** between **São Vicente** and **Porto Moniz.**

There is a viewpoint of the waterfall for which you have to leave your car in the small parking lot.

Serra do agua

The basket carts do Monte

In Funchal, along the Caminho do Comboio, an impressive descent is made with a wicker basket cart driven exclusively by two men (carreiros) with their feet and reaches up to 80 km/hour. They travel 2 km in about 10 minutes. This form of transportation was used since 1850 and today it has become a tourist attraction on the island.

The Island of Flowers

To get around Madeira, it is best to rent a car without a driver or take a jeep tour to know the nature of the island.

Boat trip or catamaran to see whales and dolphins.
Eating out in Madeira: €20 per person, lunch and dinner, per day.
Car rental in Madeira: The average cost for a day of car rental is €15 per day.

What to eat in Madeira?
Its most traditional dishes are **fish caldeirada**, **limpets** or **veal skewered in pau de lauro.**
The bread called **bolo de caco,** and the **poncha**, a cocktail made with white rum, lemon juice and honey cane.

Espetada
Grilled veal skewers with bay leaf.

Espada
Fish that is only found in the waters of Madeira.

Lapas (Limpets)
They are prepared on the grill with a squeeze of lemon.

Lulas
Clams.

Cocoa cake
Round bread made with flour, sweet potato, yeast, water and salt.
Fresh from the oven, garlic butter is spread on it.

Restaurants

-Adega da Quinta in Funchal.
To try espetada in pau de lauro and enjoy live traditional music.

-Fajã Dos Padres (Two Fathers)
The Fajã Dos Padres restaurant can only be reached by boat or by descending the cliff in a funicular, a unique and unforgettable experience.
It is located on a beautiful pebble beach surrounded by orchards and fruit fields.

-Quinta Do Furao in Santana.
Located on some cliffs on the **northeast coast**.

Pingo Doce
If you want the cheapest on the island, here you can take the food

already prepared, it is bought by weight, you only have to weigh it and pay for it.

For €15, 2 people can eat, including desserts and drinks.

New Year Celebrations

The pyrotechnic show that takes place in Madeira on New Year's Eve is world famous, considered the largest in the world, since rockets are launched from all corners of the island. The best places to see this unique spectacle are from a cruise ship, at the **Funchal Marina** or at the **Pico dos Barcelos.**

Viewpoint Salão de Baixo

Author's review

The author, a Law graduate and lover of History and classical culture, has published on Kindle an extensive collection of works dedicated to cities and monuments in Spain and the city of Rome, among which we can highlight:

-Rome and its monuments.

-Rome Travel Guide.Discover the City.

-Vatican: Travel Guide.

-All Naples.Travel Guide.

-Pompeii, Herculaneum.Travel Guide.

-The Prado easy Museum. Guide not to get lost between the pictures.

-Barcelona and its monuments.Travel Guide.

-Walking through Madrid.Get to know the city step by step.

-Walking through Madrid, Aranjuez, El Escorial, Toledo, Segovia.

-Walking through Cordova and Granada.

-Seville, Cordova and Granada.Travel Guide.

-Granada, travel guide: monuments, history, curiosities, legends.

-Toledo, travel guide: monuments, history, curiosities, legends.

-Avila, a medieval jewel, travel guide.

-The Route of Don Quixote.The Mills of La Mancha.

-Segovia and The Granja Palace:Travel Guide.

-La Palma Island, Land of Volcanoes
  Paradise under the clouds.

-Lanzarote, Paradise of Water, Sand and Fire

-Fuerteventura, Playas, Volcanes y Dunas.

THANKS

-https://es.m.wikipedia.org/wiki/Archivo:Fortaleza_do_Pico_-_147
40646014_-_2014-05-13.jpg
https://www.flickr.com/photos/79721788@N00/14740646014/A
utor D-Stanley
-https://en.m.wikipedia.org/wiki/File:São_Tiago_fortress_in_Func
hal,_Madeira.PNG.Mathiasrex Maciej Szczepańczyk
-https://en.m.wikipedia.org/wiki/File:Forte_de_S._Tiago.jpg
posted to Flickr as 2007.Author Jens karlsson
-https://commons.m.wikimedia.org/wiki/File:Câmara_de_Lobos_-
Portugal(323962381).jpg
Vitor Oliveira from Torres Vedras, Portugal.
-https://es.m.wikipedia.org/wiki/Archivo:Cabo_Girão,_Madeira.PN
G.Mathiasrex Maciej Szczepańczyk
-https://es.m.wikipedia.org/wiki/Archivo:Ribeira_Brava_5.JPG
Koshelyev
-https://es.m.wikipedia.org/wiki/Archivo:Laurissilva_da_Madeira_
13.jpg.Luismiguelrodrigues
-https://hu.m.wikipedia.org/wiki/Fájl:Boca_Encumeada.jpg.Pásztö
rperc a(z) magyar Wikipédia projektből
-https://upload.wikimedia.org/wikipedia/commons/6/61/Levada_
do_Caldeirão_Verde%2C_Madeira_-_Aug_2012_-_05.jpg.Flickr.Aut
hor cudi
-https://commons.m.wikimedia.org/wiki/File:Fortaleza_de_São_J
oão_Baptista_do_Pico,_Funchal,_Madeira_-_IMG_8709.jpg.PESP/
Wikimedia
-https://es.m.wikipedia.org/wiki/Archivo:Madeira_-_Serra_De_Agu

a_(33192222750).jpg
Autor muffinn from Worcester, UK
-https://es.m.wikipedia.org/wiki/Archivo:Paragliding_at_Arco_da_
Calheta_-_Madeira_2009.jpg
Author Claudio Vosti.Posted to Flickr by DarwIn .
-https://pt.m.wikipedia.org/wiki/Ficheiro:PecherySaoVicente.JPG
Koshelyev
-https://commons.m.wikimedia.org/wiki/File:Sao_Vicente,_Madeir
a,_Portugal,_June-July_2011_-_panoramio_(3).jpg.Author anagh
https://web.archive.org/web/20161023090052/http://www.panor
amio.com/photo/57673824
https://commons.m.wikimedia.org/wiki/File:São_Vicente_-_panor
amio.jpg.Author Jan Uyttebroeck
https://web.archive.org/web/20161010181102/http://www.panor
amio.com/photo/3942892
-https://commons.m.wikimedia.org/wiki/File:Santa_Cruz_-_Madei
ra,_2012-10-24_(07).jpg.Author Vix_B
Flickr : Madeira 2012
-https://commons.m.wikimedia.org/wiki/File:Santa_Cruz_-_Madei
ra,_2012-10-24_(08).jpg.Author Vix_B
Flickr : Madeira 2012
-https://commons.m.wikimedia.org/wiki/File:Santa_Cruz,_Madeir
a_-_2013-01-11_-_86227541.jpg
Santa Cruz, Madeira, Portugal.Maximovich Nikolay
-https://commons.m.wikimedia.org/wiki/File:Santa_Cruz,_Madeir
a_-_2013-01-11_-_86227535.jpg
Maximovich Nikolay
-https://commons.m.wikimedia.org/wiki/File:Sonnenaufgang_in_
Santa_Cruz,_Madeira.jpg

Holger Uwe Schmitt
-https://commons.m.wikimedia.org/wiki/File:2010-03-01_14_43_2
7_Portugal-Ponta_do_Pargo.jpg
Author Hansueli Krapf
-https://commons.m.wikimedia.org/wiki/File:Miradouro_de_Salão
_de_Baixo_-_Madeira,_October_2012_(1).jpg.Flickr : Madeira
2012.Author Vix_B
-https://commons.m.wikimedia.org/wiki/File:Farol_do_Pargo_(53
56819368).jpg.senza senso from Moscow, Russua
-https://pt.m.wikipedia.org/wiki/Ficheiro:Ponta_de_São_Lourenço
_north_north_east.jpg.Richard Bartz
-https://commons.m.wikimedia.org/wiki/File:Levada_do_Caniçal,_
Parque_Natural_da_Madeira_-_2018-04-08_-_IMG_3363.jpg.Paulo
SP/ Wikimedia
-https://en.m.wikipedia.org/wiki/File:XrystosSpasytelGarajau.JPG.
Koshelyev
https://es.m.wikipedia.org/wiki/Archivo:Pico_Ruivo.jpg r Kogo
-https://en.m.wikipedia.org/wiki/File:Pico-do-Arieiro-2013.JPG.Au
thor Bjørn Christian Tørrissen
http://bjornfree.com/galleries.html
-https://upload.wikimedia.org/wikipedia/commons/9/9b/2012_P
orto_Moniz.jpg.Ladislaus Hoffner
-https://commons.m.wikimedia.org/wiki/File:Arco_de_São_Jorge,
Madeira-_2009-06-26.jpg
Flickr : Madeira: North Coast.Author Jean & Nathalie
-https://en.m.wikipedia.org/wiki/File:Balcoes03.jpg
Ramessos
-https://commons.m.wikimedia.org/wiki/File:Paesaggio_dell'isola.
jpg.Moxmarco

-https://commons.m.wikimedia.org/wiki/File:Blick_auf_calheta_m
adeira_-_panoramio.jpg.azoren66
https://web.archive.org/web/20161103093807/http://www.panor
amio.com/photo/133589724
-https://es.m.wikipedia.org/wiki/Archivo:CurralDasFreiras-2013.J
PG.Autor Bjørn Christian Tørrissen
http://bjornfree.com/galleries.html
-https://es.m.wikipedia.org/wiki/Archivo:Madeira_Nordküste_8.JP
G.Cookaa
-https://es.m.wikipedia.org/wiki/Archivo:Bolo_do_caco_acabadin
hos_de_cozer.jpg. Ana Cake Design
-https://commons.m.wikimedia.org/wiki/File:Ponta_Do_Sol_Cine
ma._-_panoramio.jpg.Jane White
https://web.archive.org/web/20161028181651/http://www.panor
amio.com/photo/102464421
-https://commons.m.wikimedia.org/wiki/File:The_rocks_hug.jpg.T
onysantosc
-https://commons.m.wikimedia.org/wiki/File:Pontadosol1.JPG
Roman Klementschitz
-https://es.m.wikipedia.org/wiki/Archivo:Forte_de_Nossa_Senhor
a_do_Amparo,_Machico,_Madeira_-_IMG_6095.jpg   PESP/
Wikimedia
-https://commons.m.wikimedia.org/wiki/File:Casa_de_divisão_de
_águas_da_Levada_de_Santa_Luzia,_Fundoa,_Funchal_-_2020-06-
06_-_IMG_5690.jpg
Author PESP/ Wikimedia
-https://commons.m.wikimedia.org/wiki/File:._._Station_%5E_Tick
et_Office._-_panoramio.jpg
https://web.archive.org/web/20161031161838/http://www.panor

amio.com/photo/127810642

Author Jane White

-https://es.m.wikipedia.org/wiki/Archivo:Levada_da_Serra_do_Fai al_(Madeira).JPG.Autor Camster2

-https://es.m.wikipedia.org/wiki/Archivo:Levada_Madeira.jpg Jörg Schmalenberger (= JOEXX)

-https://es.m.wikipedia.org/wiki/Archivo:Desde_el_torreón_del_%2 2Museu_de_Fotografia_da_Madeira%22._Vista_de_Funchal,_Made ira,_Portugal.jpg

CARLOS TEIXIDOR CADENAS

-https://commons.m.wikimedia.org/wiki/File:2016_Costa_de_Fun chal._Madeira_Portugal-10.jpg

Luis Miguel Bugallo Sánchez (Lmbuga)

-https://commons.m.wikimedia.org/wiki/File:Poinsettia_(2454723 7231).jpg. muffinn from Worcester, UK

-https://commons.m.wikimedia.org/wiki/File:Madeira_-_Jardim_d o_Mar_-_Angels'_Trumpets_(24333940760).jpg.muffinn from Worcester, UK

-https://commons.m.wikimedia.org/wiki/File:Madeira_-_Calheta_- _Jardim_Do_Mar_(4733022666).jpg

Michael Gaylard from Horsham, UK

-https://commons.m.wikimedia.org/wiki/File:Madeira_-_Jardim_d o_Mar_-_View_from_the_hill_top_(24001474744).jpg.muffinn from Worcester, UK

-https://an.m.wikipedia.org/wiki/Imachen:CestoMadeira.JPG Koshelyev

-https://es.m.wikipedia.org/wiki/Archivo:Palácio_de_São_Lourenç o,_Funchal,_Madeira_-_IMG_2614.jpg PESP/ Wikimedia

-https://commons.m.wikimedia.org/wiki/File:2011-03-05_03-13_

Madeira_054_Funchal,_Sé_do_Funchal.jpg.Flickr : 2011-03-05
03-13 Madeira 054 Funchal, Sé do Funchal.Author Allie_Caulfield
-https://commons.m.wikimedia.org/wiki/File:Sé_Catedral,_Funcha
l_-_2020-05-11_-_IMG_5598.jpg
PESP/ Wikimedia
-https://commons.m.wikimedia.org/wiki/File:2012-10-25_17-58-2
5_Pentax_JH_(49281544308).jpg
Jan Helebrant
-https://commons.m.wikimedia.org/wiki/File:Funchal_Kathedrale_
Hauptaltar.jpg.Hajotthu
-https://commons.m.wikimedia.org/wiki/File:Jardim_Botanico_2_
(Funchal)_(37389127434).jpg
VillageHero from Ulm, Germany
-https://commons.m.wikimedia.org/wiki/File:2010-03-05_12_43_5
8_Portugal-Jardim_Botânico_da_Madeira.jpg.Hansueli Krapf
-https://es.m.wikipedia.org/wiki/Archivo:Palácio_dos_Cônsules,_F
unchal,_Madeira_-_IMG_6720.jpg
PESP/ Wikimedia
-https://es.m.wikipedia.org/wiki/Archivo:Levada_Caldeirao_Verde
_(Madeira).JPG.Bernard Leprêtre.
-https://es.m.wikipedia.org/wiki/Archivo:Madeira_Cascata_do_Ve
u_da_Noiva.jpg.Unukorno
-https://en.m.wikipedia.org/wiki/File:Museu_CR7_Funchal_2016.J
PG.Abby M.
-https://en.m.wikipedia.org/wiki/File:Santa_Catarina_Park_-_2014-
07-23.jpg
https://www.flickr.com/photos/79721788@N00/14724096754/A
uthor D-Stanley
-https://en.m.wikipedia.org/wiki/File:Market_funchal_hg.jpg.Hann

es Grobe

-https://commons.m.wikimedia.org/wiki/File:Casa_Colombo_Colu mbus_House_-_Vila_Baleira_-_Porto_Santo_(Portugal)_(2180443749).jpg

This image was originally posted to Flickr by Portuguese_eyes at https://flickr.com/Tm

-https://es.m.wikipedia.org/wiki/Archivo:Museu_Quinta_das_Cruzes,_Funchal,_Madeira_-_IMG_8415.jpg   Autor PESP/

Wikimedia.posted to Flickr as Holiday Madeira New Year 08-09 IMG_73

Author Mark Woodbury

-https://commons.m.wikimedia.org/wiki/File:Pipas_de_vinho_Madeira.jpg

Flickr as Holiday Madeira New Year 08-09 IMG_73

Autor Mark Woodbury

-https://es.m.wikipedia.org/wiki/Archivo:Tropical_garden_monte_hg.jpg.Hannes Grobe

-https://es.m.wikipedia.org/wiki/Archivo:Seixal_-_Madeira_01.jpg. H. Zell

-https://es.m.wikipedia.org/wiki/Archivo:25_Fontes.jpg.Eric Wüstenhagen

-https://commons.m.wikimedia.org/wiki/File:2010-03-03_18_53_16_Portugal-Seixal.jpg.Hansueli Krapf

-https://an.m.wikipedia.org/wiki/Imachen:Madère_057.jpg Gérard Janot

-https://an.m.wikipedia.org/wiki/Imachen:Santana_Madere.jpg Félix Potuit

-https://an.m.wikipedia.org/wiki/Imachen:Traditional_thatched_houses_(palheiros),_Santana,_Madeira,_Portugal.jpg

Posted to Flickr.Autor Paul Mannix
-https://es.m.wikipedia.org/wiki/Archivo:Rocha_do_Navio.jpg
Posted to Flickr as Madeia.Leo-setä
-https://commons.m.wikimedia.org/wiki/File:Ilha_de_Porto_Santo
_-_Portugal_(1524370982).jpg.Vitor Oliveira from Torres Vedras,
PORTUGAL.

Printed in Great Britain
by Amazon